Another
101 Poems from my
Lithuanian Soul
that Seek to be Sung

By: Steve Rincavage

Printing/Distribution by Steve Rincavage

Category: Poetry

© 2007 by Steve Rincavage.

ISBN 978-0-6151-8335-0

First printing, December 2007.

Front and back cover design by Perry Dollar, Brandon Rhae and Steve Rincavage.

Map of Lithuania and coat of arms from public domain.

www.lulu.com/srincavage

Also by Steve Rincavage

Dang Valley: Beginnings

101 Poems from my Lithuanian Soul that Seek to be Sung

Dedication

To anyone who's been through hell and came back to acquire a new desire.

Acknowledgements

To my passions, I give drive

To my places, I give precious memories

To my faith, I give praise

To my patterns, I give colored collages

To my blues and country, I give hope

To my details, I give a microscope

To my sports, I give energy

To my love and relationships, I give special feelings

To my nature, I give tingles

To my science, I give truth and logic

To my nonsense, I give nuts

To my poemplanations, I give my Lithuanian soul.

Special thanks to Molly and Emily Rincavage for finding my many mistakes.

Contents:

Index of poems:

Science

Nonsense

Epilogue

Map of Lithuania and my coat of arms.

Also serves as an x-ray image of my soul at birth.

Lithuania shares a similar geometric shape as Africa, go figure.

Introduction

Even though many of these words reflect to a time decades old, 98.6% were written in 2007. They came out easy after recounting the memories. There's always an age of something. There's the Stone Age, the Bronze Age, the Iron Age, the Industrial Age and the Information Age. But most of all, there is the Age of Uncertainty.

Now in order to carry it out fully, you have to be careful that you don't paint yourself into a corner. You have to depend on people to watch your back. If not, you might be left in a potato sack hangin' from a meat pack.

Sometimes u might be watching your favorite event and acid reflux hits ya when you least expect it. Visions of thorny crowns and paramecium intermingle in a mellow yellow while you envision your golden years. U try to figure it all out but you know your dreams at night are too insane to make u germane.

Once ya think you're the chosen ones, grow some wings and join the drones. Conformance is always a choice. Do I join that band or this band? Who has the greatest songs that will fill my soul with a desired goal? Where can I find patterns and texture that will provide me with bountiful nrg.

Quite honestly, I don't know what I'd do if both halves of my brain weren't in some kind of harmony. I'd probably be in a prison cell with dudes who had no proper upbringin'. I would love to run down the street like a Mississippi hippie and hand out olive branches to all those mean son of a bitches. I would pull them out of their tunnel of disdain. I would tell them, 'I got your back and there is much to gain in the mystic rain.'

So hope floats in a castle moat and you're off to the races. When some people get older, they get darker and more starker. Some folks ease up and reflect on the good times and change the world into a more soluble space. This goes from John Wesley Powell and Bill Gates to Heaven's Gate. Be a risk taker. Be a history maker.

When you're goin' to and fro, find your groove and don't be surprised if ya have to compromise to inhale the real know.

> Some people live in a distant disguise
> Tellin' all their friends such terrible lies
> Only if they knew what was in the fries
> They would find a way to compromise

> Churchill said to never compromise
> His values were much too wise
> From all the rubble and cries came a new rise
> Democracy won out to be the prize

Some people live with the fruit flies
Sheddin' all their wings into another guise
If they only knew what happens when liberty dies
They would find a way to compromise.

Everyone has a thing, a bling and their favorite ding-a-ling. What's the difference between a C sharp and a D flat? Perception my friend.

Some people live in the material world while others live in the spiritual world. Some people like to mix their drinks with coke and whiskey. I like to mix mine with faith and science. This collection of poemplanations, the convergence of poems with explanations and mixed rice, is my Lithuanian wall-banger on ice.

1. Passions

You Can Change the World

By changin' your mind, you can change your outlook
By changin' your outlook, you can change your attitude
By changin' your attitude, you can change your fortitude
By changin' your fortitude, you can change your life
By changin' your life, you can change the world

By focusin' your mind, you can pinpoint your outlook
By focusin' your outlook, you can pinpoint your attitude
By focusin' your attitude, you can pinpoint your fortitude
By focusin' your fortitude, you can pinpoint your life
By focusin' your life, you can change the world

By givin' your mind, you can live your outlook
By givin' your outlook, you can live your attitude
By givin' your attitude, you can live your fortitude
By givin' your fortitude, you can live your life
By givin' your life, you can change the world.

Inspiration came from my phlebotomist who was suckin' blood out of my arm one day. I looked up and saw a similar set of quotations hangin' on her spiritual wall. This was my take on the whole wide world of passions and spirits.

Passion

Focus and meditation made a pact with me
While walkin' thru a troubled society
I looked to the left and saw dark forests
I looked to the right and I believed in you

Chorus
If ya have style, ya have fashion
If you have guts, you have passion
If ya have guile, your hun is well done
If you have nuts, you have passion

Whoever takes that burnin' desire
Whoever likes to make a fire
They're the ones that will make you coo
They're the ones that will envelope you.

By usin' your passion, you can rearrange the world. W. Clement Stone once said, 'There is very little difference in people. But that little difference makes a big difference. The little difference is attitude. The big difference is whether it is positive or negative.' Amen.

Believe

Women walkin' down the city street lookin' at their reflection
Checkin' their hair and hour-glass figures
I've never seen one of them look the other way
Like a deer in headlights, that's what gets their attention

Steam comin' out of the manholes
Workers buildin' high-risers that reach to the sky
Ah, they look forward to the penthouse 33 floors up high
They look at the women checkin' on their reflections

When the sun comes out the women's clothes get less
Leavin' one's imagination a mess to coalesce
Ah, they look so forward to the penthouse up high
Workers buildin' high-risers that reach to the sky

These Baltimore streets have signs everywhere I turn
They tell me to Believe in big, bold letters
Ah, I Believe in the workers buildin' them high-risers
And the women checkin' their reflections on every corner.

I never worked in a metropolis until recently. It was then I noticed the mirror
phenomenon. Next time you're in a big, mirrored city, take a look, you'll see what
I'm talkin' about.

The Pros and Cons to Everything

There are Pros and Cons to everything
There are Pros and Cons to bein' a king
There are Pros and Cons that will make you sing
There are Pros and Cons that will make you sting

There are Pros and Cons to the whole lot
There are Pros and Cons to makin' an ink dot
There are Pros and Cons that make your brain clot
There are Pros and Cons that will make you rot

There are Pros and Cons for everyone
There are Pros and Cons to havin' some fun
There are Pros and Cons that will make you run
There are Pros and Cons that will make you well done

There are Pros and Cons to every situation
There are Pros and Cons to rulin' a nation
There are Pros and Cons that will bring some trepidation
There are Pros and Cons that will bring some needed elation.

Do you take into consideration the prime directive in these scenarios? Do you say the needs of the many outweigh the needs of the one or the few? Ya can't make everyone happy; trust your instincts.

Planes, Trains and Automobiles

Planes, Trains and Automobiles
They put the motion in me
I get a new perspective at 20,000 feet
Through the clouds I unwind in my seat

Wings, Whistles and Wheels
They put the feelin' of Johnny Cash in me
I get my kicks at the rail station
I ride iron and steel to my next destination

Planes, Trains and Automobiles
They put a smile on me
I go my own way in my Chevrolet
The wheels spin and rarely stray

Wings, Whistles and Wheels
They take a burden off of me
I ride in the sun with the masses
Moving bodies from all kinds of classes.

Dedicated to the train songs of Johnny Cash and that lonesome whistle only a true hobo could appreciate.

Bring it On

She's as complex as a '67 cabernet
Twists around everythin' I say
So I untwist back the sauvignon
And say, 'Come on baby, Bring it On'

God made them red grapes
I just picked and produced the body
So I untwist my king kong
And say, 'Come on baby, Bring it On'

I'm just a country calamity ya see
I don't have to talk to be merry
So I untwist my thoughts oh so long
And say, 'Come on baby, Bring it On'

I heard the weight guesser at the carnival say
'You got a lot of junk in your trunk!'
So I untwist my grin that was oh so wrong
And say, 'Come on baby, Bring it On!'

I'm sure you've been to the carnival with the carnie guessing the weight of the passers by once they fork up their hard-earned dough. There's always that one patron the carnie walks around, contently stares at their buttocks and shouts on his headset, 'You got a lot of junk in your trunk!' I'm sorry, but that's raw entertainment ya just can't find anywhere else.

Be Prepared

Once a scout, always a scout
To Akela's light, this is no doubt

There is a scout law, 'I will be
Trustworthy, Loyal, Helpful, Friendly,
Courteous, Kind, Obedient, Cheerful,
Thrifty, Brave, Clean and Reverent.'

There is another spirit out there
So listen up here:

'May the Spirit of Scouting
And the Light of Akela
Be with you and me
Until our paths
Cross Again.'

Some folks turn to their Bible in times of terror
Some folks tip the bottle in their times of trouble
I like to turn to the 12 scout laws and Akela
When I need somethin' more than a common cure.

Be prepared, in my opinion, one of the best organizations around to promote value lessons for life. Just ask anyone who has spent a lot of time in the blue and gold.

John Wesley Powell

He walked across Wisconsin at twenty-one
Just cause it was there
He lost his right arm at Shiloh
A Civil War casualty that said let's row, row, row

The one-armed river runner who did his number
With balls the size of the Grand Canyon
Enough to lead a pack of nine adventurous men
In 1869 goin' aroun' every Colorado river bend

Three men got scared and set off on their own
Never to see Powell and his men again
Some say it was Shevwits Indians, others say the Mormons
I say it was fate that killed them in their delirium

Chorus
The one-armed balls runner made it through
An exploration of huge magnitude
The Southwest was chartered in manifest destiny
Left the rest up to society and you and me

He became an advocate of geology
It's no wonder given his history
It was there to be conquered
By a one-armed balls runner who never blurred.

JWP is one of my heroes. When I get scared, I think of this man facin' his fears.
His crew started out on May 24, 1869 and on August 30th made it to the mouth of
Virgin River. It was a trek of 1,048 miles through some of the most rugged country
left on this planet to explore. Four men quit of which three were never seen again.
When I think of men with big kahoonas, the one-armed river runner is at the top of
my list.

This Side of the Dirt

Like a canary in a coal mine
I checked the air to see if it was still fine
I came by to give her some red wine
Once she drank it, we began to dine

Like a dog in a wolf pack
I looked to circle my prey today
Like a cat on a night hunt
I looked to rub my paws on you

Chorus
I'm still on this side of the dirt
But I can still feel your primal hurt
I'll never let you down
Even when I'm six feet underground

Like a bum in a dumpster
Everybody has to find their way
I came by to give her some sweet divine
Once she believed it, she became mine.

When you are on this side of the dirt, the physical takes over the logical. When you are on the other side of the dirt, the spirit takes over the physical. Hopefully your dirt allows children and plants to flourish in your afterlife.

2. Places

Maine

When the days turn longer
I long for the North Woods of Maine
If you've been there ya know what I mean
The moose, mountains and water make a precious scene

If ya journey up to the North Woods
Ya better bring your memory to capture the goods
Cause this way of life may one day may be no more
Katahdin's rocks weep at the thought of this

When the days turn longer
I long for the paths and rocks of Acadia
If you've been there ya know what I mean
The ocean, rocks and lobster make a precious scene

If ya journey up to the North Woods
Ya better bring your memory to capture the goods
Cause this way of life may one day may be no more
Acadia's paths weep at the thought of this.

They don't call it Vacationland for nothin'. Acadia, Penebscot, Pollywog Pond
and Katahdin all have a magical fate in my fifty-first natural state.

White Mountain Glory

There's a presidential range in the Whites
They divide the day into the night
Rugged and jagged and rugged all over
Leavin' your soul in need of some shelter

This is a place where weather likes to congregate
And create a place of a six-foot under fate
Just look at the wall of all those who perished
When tryin' to conquer its weathered stone

These mountains don't give up the dead
I know this from feelin' its rocky bed
I know this from seein' its ravens soar
I know this from the winds blowin' through

If ya can make it to Tuckerman Ravine
Ya swear it's the Swiss Alps you've seen
Just make sure ya have your wits to survive
Or you'll end up on the wall of tragedy.

When I search my mind for some of the most intense feelings I have for Mother
Nature, the White Mountains come to the top of the list. Ya can be explorin' its
crevices in July and die of hypothermia. It was August when I inhaled its fog at
Tuckerman's Ravine and I saw the divine. If it wasn't for those AMC huts,
who knows, I may have ended up on the wall of those who perished in White
Mountain glory.

Central Park

While I'm in the middle of Central Park
I'm so at peace, it's like a paradox
A concrete jungle surrounds me
Yet I'm surrounded by such beauty

I've got trees to my left
Green pasture to my right
God dang these rocks and ponds are a sight
Let's get a picnic basket and eat here tonight

The high-rises stand like mountains in the distance
Shootin' reflections of light in all directions
North, South, East and West
Central Park has the space to promote a rest

When you need to find peace in the big city
Look for Central Park and bring your favorite book
Invite your lover and spend time under the covers
The trees will shade you from the stress and bad press.

I've only been to Central Park twice, but it's such a fascinatin' space. Talk about contrast. Most people spend their time on Fifth Avenue lookin' at all the revenue and feelin' blue. I like to go to Central Park and look for the artists, movements and musicians feelin' free in the state of the Statue of Liberty.

Mississippi Hippie

He was a Mississippi hippie
Who took life a little zippy

They thought he was a vandal with sandals
Just cause he sucked on a fat dill pickle
Tossin' his 1967 summer of love nickle
While doin' the Mississippi Half-Step toodeloo

He was a Mississippi hippie
Who took life a little trippy

He said that peace, love and long hair
Are all that really matters to him
Mississippi hippie's real name was Jumpin' Ely
All laid out in a tie-dye tee shirt sippin' some rock n' rye

He was a Mississippi hippie
Who took life a little zippy

That hippie loved to get on that river boat
And smoke them Cuban cigars
While eatin' his fat dill pickles
That was one fine divine Mississippi hippie

He was a Mississippi hippie
Who took life a little trippy.

Inspiration came from watchin' a Boy Scout skit in Virginia. One of the
characters was a Mississippi Hippie. This is my version of my Mississippi
Hippie with a little Jerry Garcia and Robert Hunter mixed in.

Also influenced by my favorite pickle hippie story from family and friends.

The Desert

Lace up them hikin' boots and head to the desert
It's about time ya absorbed a *k*new perspective
If you don't get one sittin' in its fold
Then go see a psychiatrist and put your life on hold

Get in that car and put her in gear
Head to where the land is brown all year
Look for the rocks chiseled by ice, wind and water
Time will alter your perspective as a starter

Get that backpack and tighten that belt
Hike to the arches and labyrinths to see what I felt
Look for the origins of what you have become
Praise your history and your future will get some

Time is a mirror when ya look into its chasms
Your mind, heart and religion will go into spasms
As you try to figure out how it all began
The profound desert, I'm your biggest fan.

Ya can look at the desert as a huge wasteland or ya can let it change your life.
It's up to you.

Southwest Quest

We planned and tanned in our Southwest Quest
Time to leave the nest while they're still at their best
Figured out we would put their mind and body to the test
Oooh we, ya better bet life will take on a new zest

So it goes somethin' like this:
Rocky Mountain National Park first in the queue
Onward to a Delicate Arch with a mind-blowin' hue
Next to Sego and Horseshoe Canyon
Marveled at petroglyphs from years well done

Down through the Capitol Reef waterpocket fold
On to Bryce Canyon where hoodoos live I'm told
Rode some mules through a fairyland so true
Went to see what a Virgin River in Zion can do

Hiked down the Grand Canyon to see if there is a Hell
It's under the Vishnu Schist, I'll give you a yell
Camped in primitive tents in a geological time scale
Ended up in El Tovar reading some e-mail

Sunset and Meteor Crater formed an impression on me
Spent the night on Route 66 in a concrete tipi
We came across fossils in Petrified Forest National Park
Noticed how the desert is so beautiful and so stark

Drove to Hubble Trading Post to get some goods
Ended up in Canyon De Chelley to examine my moods
They were pretty high on the way to Four Corners
Stuck each appendage in a state and prayed for the mourners

There at Mesa Verde up in the cliffs it dawned on me
How much nature can feed my reality
Ended up at the plaza in downtown Santa Fe
There at Loretto Chapel it came to me in a light ray

Came back to the old east coast we call home
Thousands of miles spent in this metallic dome
Ended up finishing with Mammoth National Park
The caves and this quest gave us a new spark.

Sooner or later, hopefully the former, you can take a quest and make it the best.

My Favorite Tool

My favorite tool is my six-foot metal shaft pry bar
Doesn't require no electricity
Doesn't require no self-pity
Just a willingness to move the pile

So when I go to the job site
I always have my six-foot metal shaft pry bar
It's near my soul so I can take the boulder on a roll
For every fulcrum there's a world of doldrums

My favorite tool is my six-foot metal shaft pry bar
Doesn't require no electricity
Doesn't require no calamity
Just a willingness to dig the hole

So when I go to sleep at night
I always dream of my six-foot metal shaft pry bar
It's near my soul so I can take the boulder on a roll
For every divot there's a world of pivots.

I was first introduced to my favorite tool while volunteering on the Appalachian Trail crew. We moved a lot of boulders durin' that trail relocation. When I returned home, I just had to have a six-foot metal shaft pry bar. I use it to move the pile, support my John Deere tractor and dig holes at my vineyard. There's nothin' better to gain leverage on that pile.

There is always a place in my heart for my dependable six-foot metal shaft pry bar. This was written to a rock beat.

Mushrooms, Coal and Pickles

My Daddy took me for a walk in his Pennsylvania woods
He showed me where he used to pick his mushrooms
Ah come on Dad, you really ate those things
Now I look back and say, 'Old man you never had it that good.'

Then he showed me where they mined the coal
Those poor son of a bitches had to risk everything
Just to extract that stuff from Mother Earth
Then black lung from deep within did them in

Our trip ended where he had cucumbers in a jar
They made themselves the greatest pickles
Ya swear God came down and blessed those things
Now I look back and say, 'Old man you never had it that good.'

One of my favorite childhood trips takin' in the woods of Plymouth, Pennsylvania.

November Wind

Here comes that northern November wind blowin' around my house
It shakes my windows and rattles my bones
It's like a funnel to an endless ding-a-ling
If I could only harness that power I would be king

Here comes that southern November wind blowin' around my house
The solar rays enter the atmosphere with little fear
Those winds from Louisiana still bite me in two
Who said the delta didn't know a thing or two about the blues

Here comes that eastern November wind blowin' around my house
The ocean knows how to create some funnels indeed
The seagulls ride them all the way to their next destination
Getting there in half the time to their next station

Here comes that western November wind blowin' around my house
Shakes my bones and rattles my windows
God dang it rattles my soul when that wind blows
Shakes my relativity and makes my nose rose.

Our current house sits on top of a hill with no trees surrounded by undulating farm land. I've noticed there is a certain tilt to this land come November cause I've never seen such a constant wind come blowin' in. One day I'm gonna figure out how to harness that thing with a fast metabolism and be a king.

3. Faith

Free Will

God created many branches from the tree of life
Gave us his son who was hung on a cross in strife
To that end we were given a choice
Embrace free will and give it a faithful voice

There's another meetin' place I do declare
It's in a time zone where everythin' is fair
No daylight savings or clock to punch you out
Just a place where angels and golden towers are about

Stay away from the hotties
Unless their brain matter matches their bodies
There's trouble brewin' in that nirvana
Leave that branch and go take a sauna

You can choose love or hate
There's nothin' left to debate
Find your peace and make it stand
Then God may lend you a helpin' hand.

A Mississippi hippie once told me free will comes in a pill. I told him hell no, free will comes from blood, sweat and tears.

John the Baptist

John the Baptist had some passion
Some say it was just a fashion
Little did they know he was a revolution
He pulled in his cousin as the solution

A rebel with a cause
A rebel with a destination
He could tell you about dungeons
He could tell you about faith

Chorus
He dipped his head
Then he went and said
If it is to be
It is up to me

John the Baptist went on a tryst
Some say it was just an open fist
Little did they know he was a revelation
He teamed with his cousin to make the separation

The locust-eater said it's the one who follows who matters
Herod delivered his holy head on a platter
His homeboy became much greater
So our sins could be forgiven later.

Salome asked her mother, Herodias, what to ask from Herod since she danced so
well. How about serving John's head on a platter she requested. A crazy way to go
for a simple, holy man filled with passion. The locust and honey eater knew he
must become less but did not see his cousin serve his final mission. One wonders if
he was there things may have been different. I have a feeling he would have laid
down his life for his homeboy unlike the other followers who fled to fill the
prophecy.

Missionary Mojo

He was Saul then became Paul
He traveled to and fro with a lot of mojo
He filled the world with words of passion
In mixed blood with a Roman fashion

He persecuted Christians in joy
Then went on to become its greatest missionary
It's a story Paul likes to mention
It's a story filled with redemption

Jesus was an outcast Jew who knew
He must obey God first and not man
He came to Paul in a blinding light
This forever changed the black of night

It's not, 'Where has God gone?'
It's, 'Where have I gone?'
So Paul once thought, 'There go I
When I see my brother go bye.'

So the story goes, you're travelin' through Syria and you get hit by a blinded light. You find out real quick the things you hate you can surprisingly love. Your false first impressions play mind tricks on you. You say to yourself, 'I better go change the world and write some letters before it changes me.'

Starting off with the stoning of Stephen, many of the early Christians were persecuted. Then came a beheaded John the Baptist, Jesus' crucifixion, Paul was imprisoned/beheaded and ten apostles were beheaded, stoned, sawed in two or crucified. Many others would be beaten to the brink of death by the Romans and other non-believers. Man can not handle unseen change on a grand scale.

70 times 7

Forgiveness is a matter of grace
That's what I learned when it comes to race
Prejudice will put a frown on your face
And the riot police shootin' the mace

He who believes in the forgiveness of sins wins
He who does not, is a robot
He who does not, will rot
He who does not, is not

70 times 7, it's very hard to do
My patience gets tested at two
It turns downright nasty down to the core
Especially to the poor, obscure and spiritually sore

She who believes in the forgiveness of sins wins
She who does not, is a robot
She who does not, will rot
She who does not, is not.

The Parable of the Unmerciful Servant (Matthew 18)

Then Peter came to Jesus and asked, 'Lord, how many times shall I forgive my brother when he sins against me? Up to seven times?'

Jesus answered, 'I tell you, not seven times, but seventy times seven times.'

The real question is what happens on the 491st time? Do you stone them? Hmmm. Don't worry, if you forgive more than three times you are probably on your way to sainthood.

Some folks think 70 x 7 = Infinity.

In summary, forgiveness isn't a matter of tallying rights and wrongs. Forgiveness is a matter of grace.

Satan (Don't let that)

Satan is fookin' with you
I can tell by the rendezvous
Of your temptation makin' you a two-tone blue
Don't let that fooker fook with you

He's just playin' with your mind
Show him you're not that kind
To sell your soul to the unsettled hue
Don't let that fooker fook with you

Satan is fookin' with you
I can tell by that rusty hook
Don't take the bait and get cooked
Don't let that fooker fook with you

He's just playin' with your mind
Show him you're not that kind
To sell your soul and get booked
Don't let that fooker fook with you.

Ode to Flip Wilson's, 'The devil made me do it.' Try to avoid that lake of fire.
The book tells us if you're one of God's elect then Satan will select his day with
you. Remember, show him who's boss, don't let the fooker fook with you.

The Cornerstone

Brick by brick
Stone by stone
Screw by screw
This structure won't leave you alone

Nail by nail
Stone by stone
Cross by cross
This structure won't leave you alone

Light by light
Stone by stone
Wire by wire
This structure won't leave you alone

Shingle by shingle
Stone by stone
Wall by wall
This structure won't leave you alone

Memory by memory
Stone by stone
Prayer by prayer
This structure won't leave you alone.

About solid foundations and the birth of a righteous nation and creation.

Patience

Let God be God
Let Nature be Nature
Let You be Yourself
There's a lure for sure in that turtle-shell core

Easy as 1, 2, 3
Make patience guide your liberty
Shutdown the impulse engine
You will go away with less sin

Let God be God
Let Nature be Nature
Let You be Yourself
There's a cure for sure in that patience rapture.

Dedicated to the wise and patient turtle.

Livin' in Heaven

I was thinkin just the other day
Maybe this place we live in is already heaven
That means we all died in a previous life and Eden is upon us
Grab that Bible and let's get on the magic bus

Would Eden allow millions to die a tragic death
My testament tells me it ain't so
But my conscience tells me, 'Hey Yo,
Don't paint yourself in a corner of Hell No!'

Livin' in Heaven where the light is bright
Some more babies joined our Nirvana brethren
How could Heaven be better than this
I travel to starvin' Africa then I get the reality hiss.

There are some days I say to myself, man how could heaven be any sweeter than this. Then a few days go by with a new sigh and I say goodbye to my utopian high.

Some mathematicians say Hell = Life without God.

Blue Spray Paint

These past twenty years I've traveled
The highways crisscrossing this great land
The strangest sight I think I've seen
Are the blue spray-painted words of *'JESUS SAVES'*

The handwriting is all the same
Michigan, Pennsylvania, Colorado, it doesn't matter
Just check the highway bridges and you'll know what I mean
This painting trickster has made his mark on me

Now I'm beginning to see there is salvation
It's been digested all over our roads
North, South, East and West
It's around every corner, every city, every town

This Merry Prankster is a religious one
And he's made his mark on me
Yes, Jesus Saves, Saves What, Saves the unknown
As we each ponder our fate in a camouflaged waste.

I had to try this myself one day so I spray painted 'Trust Dod' on a bridge near me.
Don't lock me up Johnny Law, it was just an experiment, and a fine one at that.

The Holy Land

There's bedlam in Bethlehem
There's newness in Nazareth
There's Jews in Jerusalem
There's Arabs in Arabia

There r syringes in Syria
There's mess ups in Mesopotamia
There's lip service in Libya
There's mercenaries in Mecca

Whatever happened to love thy neighbor?
How quickly it became an undone favor
There's holy in the Holy Land
But there are one too many bombs layin' in the sand

There's Noah at the advent ark
There's Moses at the burning bush
There's Jesus at the welcoming wilderness
There's weeping at the wailin' wall

There's bedlam in Bethlehem
There's newness in Nazareth
There's pressure in Palestine
There's holes in the Holy Land

Whatever happened to love thy neighbor?
How quickly it became an undone favor
There's holy in the Holy Land
But there are one too many bombs sinkin' in quicksand.

I often wonder if persecution and paradox will ever leave Persia. Who is going to compromise first? In my eyes, if a religion can't find a way to compromise with other rational faiths, then flush it down the toilet and walk away.

Religious Thoughts

Temperament is highly inheritable
Prejudices and retaliation become unbearable
God does have a sense of humor
So it goes with greed in that unrighteous tumor

I godda be me cause everybody else was taken
That's what I was told when the earth was shakin'
God will not legislate your love for the holy spirit
Just dance over this way and provide him a pirouette

Chorus
For a good time, call God
For a high time, call the Force
For a nice time, call Allah
For a sense of purpose, call the Higher Ground

Perfectionist vs. the Humblest
Each one tugs at the heart
Jesus was the only one to be perfect
So it's okay to be a humble sinner in dialect

God made his chosen people flee, why not you and me
Life isn't easy when you're travelin' in melancholy misery
If you have no faith then Satan will have his day with you
Why you ask, cause I've seen it first hand in my blues.

God also has a sense of blowin' stuff up. I heard a preacher say we are all bonded in the same way, that each of us came from a mother. Made me think of the future where babies may not have mothers. Also made me think of a new religion called One, where folks quantify and denounce the curses of fanatics and jealousy.

Coincidence or Fate?

Coincidence or Fate?
That's what we're here to debate
Pure chance or destiny?
What side of the fence is your reality?

Coincidence or Fate?
Wait to open the gate mate
Pot luck or providence?
What side of the border is your reality?

Coincidence or Fate?
That's what we're here to debate
Darwinism or Divine intervention?
What side of the line is your reality?

Coincidence or Fate?
Do you have the guts to not hate
Deflection or unbridled suspension?
What side of the fight is your reality?

There have been things in my life that I can only contribute to one thing and that is fate. I'm sure others like rage would argue otherwise, but this is my reality.

4. Patterns

Déjà vu

I turned around by the majestic oak tree
It was there that I said to myself in me,
'I've been here before where the wind blew anew
It was that deep feelin' of a mysterious déjà vu.'

Chorus
Déjà vu if ya only knew
What ya did to me
Set me on a self-examination
To believe in the holy reincarnation

I went to see my windy city where the breezes flew
I drove by some cows and knew their time was due
To take a walk down the gallows and moo, moo, moo
It was that deep feelin' of a mysterious déjà vu

Déjà vu if ya only knew
What ya did to me
Set me on a self-examination
To believe in the holy reincarnation.

I know folks who go to Gettysburg's battlefields and see orbs and ghosts. Others feel they have been on the battlefield before and have a connection to the bloody gore. If you haven't had a déjà vu experience, try a happy rendezvous and unglue everything you once knew.

Less is More

Every equation has a symbol from man
Sometimes equal,
Sometimes less than or
Many times greater than

If ya match both sides of the equation
You'll leave a balance for the next generation

If ya point the arrow to the left
You'll leave leftovers for the next generation

If ya point the arrow to the right
You'll leave righteousness for the next generation.

Did God create math or did man?   Some would say since God created man, he had
to create math. Others would say math only came about in the last million years
and was brought forth by man. I say dinosaurs new the importance of counting to
three seconds when playing survival hide and seek.

Yo!

Yo!

Always been a dream of mine to create a one word, red white and blue American poem. It was a tough choice between Equilibrium, Paradox, Supercalifragilisticexpialidocious and Yo. I thought Yo painted a Betsy Ross colored canvas and let one's imagination and actions form a freedom rainbow.

Yo, this is for Beau, Rocky and Adrian. It's also for the three hundred nationalities compacted into New York City that came up with one word to change a city and a country.

Immigrant

I'm just a Lithuanian immigrant
I've got my pickles, mushrooms and honey bees
I spin my basketball while lookin' at the trees
My Chicago slaughterhouse was an ugly stint

I'm just a Polish immigrant
I've got my people to pull me thru
I build my ships from steel and pig iron
My poles point north when I start to pant

I'm just a German immigrant
I've got my beer and wine so fine
I turn my imperfections to walk the line
My cows got milk and that's no stunt

I'm just a Lithuanian immigrant
I'm just a Polish immigrant
I'm just a German immigrant
Ya can't deny my hunt to be a European immigrant.

American immigrant, is that what you call yourself? Hmm. Well not me, I'm a Lithuanian, Polish and German immigrant from Ellis Island with an East Coast Mint.

Mistaken Identity

I thought you were him but I was wrong
It was a case of mistaken identity
My senses lost all their rationality
I'm so sorry, please accept my heartfelt apology

My memory is shot and that's a fact
Got too much nonsense stuffed intact
Need to empty the trash and make some space
Nothin' to do but replace my mistaken face

It was a case of mistaken identity
I thought you were him but I was wrong
Now all I have left is my tattered song
I need a drum stick and a big, loud gong.

Given the fact that humans are genetically very similar. I submit there are many cases of mistaken identity every day. I had a bizarre case with some identical twins and a few others to report on along the way.

I wonder if chimps have the same problem.

The Haves and Have Nots

I ride two trains to work
One to Baltimore three days a week
The other to DC to take on the meek
I notice one of them has the Haves
And the other one has the Have Nots

The DC Haves are dressed up nice
The Baltimore Have Nots have their Bibles
One's got designer clothes that are superficial
The other has rags that are filled with desire

The DC Haves have white collars and ties
The Baltimore Have Nots have their hard hats
One's got politics on their mind
The other has, 'What can my baby eat today?'

I ride two trains to work
One to Baltimore and feel their pain
The other to DC and feel their disdain
I notice one of them has the Haves
And the other one has the Have Nots.

It's an interestin' comparison: DC Train metro riders vs. Baltimore metro riders. Ya can't help but notice the disparity. One has the movers and shakers, both have the beggars and takers.

Jamais Content

It was the winter of our discontent
The grapes or wrath were among us
I read every Steinbeck novel I could find
Oklahoma Dust to Salinas, here comes the grind

Every good winemaker tries to find the balance
Too much stress and the grape will undress
Not enough stress and the grape will not ripen unless
Every good winemaker finds that balance

Chorus
Quelle heure est cela?
Le temps pour faire le vin
How I'm bent on you Jamais Content
How I meant to follow you

Don't conform to the masses
Take a respite on those passes
Your time in the sun will come
It's just a matter of timing.

Every good winemaker has a credo. Jamais content is no exception. It means they know a better wine can be made. It means accepting new ideas. It means not getting lazy and conforming to the status quo.

Supply vs. Demand

Even Steven was down at the shore
Thinkin' about balance and pictures
He thought about supply and demand
It was then he knew all about the sand

Even Steven joined a circle of economists
Thinkin' about micro and macro models
He thought about supply and demand
It was then he knew about the ragtime band

Even Steven was hung-over on all the theories
Thinkin' about Adam Smith and the green dollar
He thought about supply and demand
It was then he knew how to increase his hand

Even Steven was predicting the future of green
Thinkin' about power of people and economies
He thought about supply and demand
It was then he knew how the rand made a stand.

The rand is hard currency from resources rich South Africa. Some predict in three hundred years this megalopolis will rule the financial world. How do I know, by lookin' at my crystal ball on my Pink Floyd wall.

Enough is Enough

'When is enough, enough?' you ask
'When innocent blood spews rivers of disgust,' I reply
Revolutions spark the disgusted to take action
Grab a rifle and get some traction

'When is enough, enough?' you ask
'When children never get past their teens,' I reply
If I had my way I'd plant them a love potion tree
But it would be fruitless endeavor given our history

'When is enough, enough?' you ask
'When judgment day is upon you,' I reply
Sorry crazed leader, that's no lie
Will you be met hastily at the gate, me oh my.

Sometimes ya have to kick some ass, sometimes it's better to go bass fishin'. No one has a crystal ball and every civilization will one day fall, count on it.

5. Blues & Country

Someone once told me, life always gets in the way of havin' fun.
Sometimes life won't even leave your shadow alone.

Fungus Among Us Blues

There's a fungus among us
It's full of puss and causin' a big fuss
It's spreadin' like a virus in heat
Its irritation has headed south to my feet

There's a fungus among us
It's traveled all this way to the bus
It's spreadin' like a cat in heat
Its irritation goes bonkers on the bus seat

There's a fungus among us
It's full of spit and causin' a big raucous
It's spreadin' like a summer in heat
Its irritation has caused me to miss my beat

There's a fungus among us
It's full of puss and causin' me to cuss
It's spreadin' like a fire in heat
Its irritation has caused me a great defeat.

Be prepared young Boy Scout, ya better wash in them crevices or else the fungus will be among us.

Poison Ivy Blues

Woke up this morning with a terrible itch
I cried out, 'Oh Lord, life can be a scratchy bitch'
I scratched and scratched but to no avail
Urushiol poison covered me to the tail

I've got them poison ivy blues
My itch is a bitch that just won't quit
I can't even think when I try to think
Cause the itchin' has taken me over the brink

Techno and Calamine lotion
I put them all on and say a magic potion
It's to no avail, I'm still itchin' my bail
I need the steroids to get me out of jail

I've got them poison ivy blues
My itch is a bitch that just won't quit
I can't even think when I try to think
Cause this itchin' is a bitchin' stink!

Another in the long line of fungus poems. 85% of Homo sapiens wish that
Toxicodendron radicans would go bye-bye. Maybe Satan planted this when he had
some power. Maybe God left it here for us sinners to humble our society and for
birds to eat to get thru winter. I know prayer and Methylprednisolone are my only
cure.

I Don't want to be your Pimp (ode to Bubbles)

I went down to the dark side of the avenue
Where pimps were hustlin' their gals in the cloudy afternoon
Bubbles took a look at me and battered her false eyelashes
I wondered if she ever got any hot flashes

Me and my co-worker ate lunch every Friday near the Block
That's where Baltimore hookers take their wares in stock
Next to the cops and bankers I wonder to myself
That pimp's got a fake limp and looks like a bling-bling she-wimp

He flashes his gold but his gal's got the goods to secure a nation
When is that pimp gonna take a permanent vacation?
Like a pusher with his dope dealin' that stealin' greasy feelin'
I wondered if this avenue ever sees the light in the evenin'.

Dedicated to all the Bubbles on E. Baltimore Street. May the wind catch those Bubbles and blow them to a land fairer then the honey dew. Reminds me of Shakedown Street: 'Don't tell me this town ain't got no heart, just gotta poke around.'

Superpower 24-Hour Heavyweight Blues

When you're a superpower
Ya try to carry the world on your shoulders
Ya try to spread your philosophies to new boulders
But the worldly boulders turn their shoulders to the wind

Your armies are spread
They're lyin' half-dead
They're lookin' way too thin
You're gonna lose if you don't win

Chorus
I've got those superpower, 24-hour heavyweight blues
Help me Lord see what's goin' down
I don't want to die in this God forsaken town
With nothin' but clowns with downtrodden frowns

If ya bite off more than you can chew
Ya got to pay the penalty
Ya can't change the unwilling
Even if ya drop missiles that sting

In the battle hour I try not to cower
I think about the Roman tower
I think about their situation so dower
Nothin' left to do this hour but plant a spring flower.

Dedicated to that soldier sweatin' bullets in a bunk hole wonderin' if they're ever
gonna see their sweetheart again. My prayers are with you soldier.

Prison Blues

In prison, there is no tomorrow
Scuffles get settled in the now
But in the free world
If not today, there's always tomorrow

Now this is what they say in cell block ten,
'Live to Die
Die to Live
Give to Live
Live to Give
Win to Lose
Lose to Win
But whatever you do, do it now.'

In prison, there is no real sorrow
If so, it's only done in the midnight hour
But in the free world
If not today, there's always tomorrow.

Go talk to someone who has spent time in prison, they'll tell you, there is no tomorrow, things get settled in the now.

Mid-Life Crisis

He's livin' in his mid-life crisis
She's livin' in her mid-wife crisis
They're both sharin' their mid-life crisis
Nothin' left to do but hiss and find bliss

They coulda, shoulda, woulda
But they didn't have the attitude
They coulda, shoulda, woulda
But they didn't have the magnitude

He's livin' in his mid-life crisis
She's livin' in her mid-wife crisis
They're both sharin' their mid-life crisis
Nothin' left to do but find them in the amiss.

When you look at life and its cup is always half empty, then you've hit your mid-life crisis. If every color of the rainbow is a faded hue and you don't have a clue, then you've hit your mid-life crisis. If your tired 24*7 and don't believe in a higher power in the midnight hour, then you've hit your mid-life crisis. If you're a Pisces, make that fish hiss.

Dedicated to all those livin' at 1313 Malfunction Junction Way.

Stop Livin' in Bitch City

Jack complains to Jill about everythin' under the sun
Never has fun in playin' well done
She's her whippin' boy toy
Whatever happened to havin' a little joy?

Jack's no angel but Jill's been hangin' with the devil
She manages to take it to another level
Her attitude toward Jack is so damn rude
Given no respect she puts Jack in a raw mood

All they want is to stop livin' in Bitch City
Every time you see them it turns into a pity
All they want is to stop livin' in Bitch City
They know deep down each is so beautiful and witty.

Bitch City is such an ugly place. Blow it up with love missiles and show that bitch who's the boss.

Coulda, Shoulda, Woulda Blues

I Coulda, Shoulda, Woulda
But I didn't have the guts, nuts and struts
I Coulda, Shoulda, Woulda
But I didn't know the color n' hue of a midnight blue

I Coulda, Shoulda, Woulda
But I didn't have the will to instill a cold chill
I Coulda, Shoulda, Woulda
But I didn't know the makeup to change the world

I Coulda, Shoulda, Woulda
But I didn't have the guts, nuts and struts
I Coulda, Shoulda, Woulda
But I didn't know the color and hue of a midnight blue

I Coulda, Shoulda, Woulda
I Coulda, Shoulda, Woulda
I Could-a, Should-a, Would-a.

I could of, should of and would of, but I hit too many buts, cuts and ruts.

Saddest Day of My Life

It started out okay
But ended in a horrendous display
Of uncontrolled sympathy
For the man who set my destiny

It was the saddest day of my life
When I received that telephone call
My thoughts ruptured when I heard the news
My own blood lay dead, my soul then bled

It was the saddest day of my life
Didn't get a chance to tell him goodbye
Didn't get a chance to tell him how
How much he put his destiny in me

It started out okay
But ended in a lost disarray
Of misaligned feelings and the piety
Dear Lord, take his soul in mercy.

Don't con me, everyone out there has a saddest day of life to remorse in.
Fortunately, we also have a happiest day of life to recall as well.

Poor Me Baby

I've been battered, I've been shattered
I've been tattered, I've been splattered
I've been nothin' but a lost cause
Oooooooh we, Poor Me Baby

I've been chattered, I've been smattered
I've been spattered, I've been scattered
I've been nothin' but a lost soul
Oooooooh we, Poor Me Baby

I've been pattered, I've been smattered
I've been clattered, even when it didn't matter
I've been nothin' but a lost man
Oooooooh we, Poor Me Baby

Oooooooh we, Poor Me Baby
Oooooooh we, Poor Me Baby
Oooooooh we, Poor Me Baby
Oooooooh we, Poor Me Baby.

When you're down and out, give a shout, poor me baby. See if anyone comes runnin' about. The Rolling Stones' Shattered was part inspiration for this one.

Three Chords and a Bottle

Three chords and a bottle of whisky
Whatever happened to pigeon-free liberty?
Three chords and a bottle of rum
Now I sit here with my guitar and strum

Three chords and a bottle of Jack
On the verge of a fatal heart attack
Three chords and a bottle of brew
I rediscovered my past and can't get my due

Three chords and a bottle of gin
My time is due, I'm full of sin
Three chords and a bottle of wine
My pickup truck and dog are my divine.

Dedicated to Hank Williams Sr. who established much of the country and blues still in motion today. Play this on your jukebox at your favorite country tavern.

Raindrop Split Blues

We were in that cloud havin' ourselves a grand 'ole time
Just one big, rollin' vapor puff livin' in the sublime
But all great puffs must come to an end
The thunder roared and gravity pulled us down

Lightnin' jettisoned and charged the ground at dawn
The mountains below said, 'Come on Puff, bring it on'
The winds grew heavy and so did the moisture in our cloud
The electrons, protons and neutrons were all on the prowl

We made it out of the cloud and were laughin' in buckets of rain
We flew through the air with all our friends in vain
Soaring like cartoon characters in suspended animation
We tasted the wind and merged with another drop or two

Our drop landed exactly at the tip and split on the Continental Divide
I headed east to the Mississippi and my brother west to the Pacific side
We barely had enough time to say good-bye on those Rocky Mountains
Little did I know it would be years before I would ever see him again

I ended up in a Denver sewage pump for months singin' the blues
I swirled in the king's toilet bowl in Memphis and cried about you
My favorite time was swimmin' with the crabs in the Gulf of Mexico
They taught me a lot about a connected universe I didn't know

My brother swam the Grand Canyon in the time of his life
He hated every minute in Vegas shootin' bullets near the neon strife
Was diverted to the Salinas Valley and met up with some lettuce
He wanted to be with the vines but they didn't need a lot of his kind

He made it to the Pacific and tasted the North Pole
Ended up gettin' shot out of a Humpback whale blow hole
Made his way through the gills of Hammerhead sharks
He said he loved the sea turtles and their demeanor the most

Years later, we met up in a terrible storm at Cape Horn
Two twenty-foot waves collided and we were re-born
We still had two hydrogen and one oxygen on our side
Then merged and reminisced all the way to Antarctica

Now we are solidified in an iceberg so cold
Seals come and lay on us, they're so bold
We think with global warming we'll hit the oceans soon
And be evaporated up into the puff and start anew.

Not sure where this one came from. Would be quite a story to track on PBS.

6. Details

Minutia

Choose your battles well
Leave nothin' left to sell
It's the details that matter
I know this dealin' with my mad hatter

In all your minutia, there is negativity
In all your minutia, there is lost creativity
In all your minutia, there is nativity
In all your minutia, there is lost spontaneity

Choose your details well
Leave nothin' left to dwell
It's the details that matter
I know this dealin' with my brain chatter

In all your minutia, there is creativity
In all your minutia, there is lost negativity
In all your minutia, there is spontaneity
In all your minutia, there is lost nativity.

If ya take all your minutia and manage it well, your life will gel.

Women and Children First

Whatever happened to women and children first?
Me oh my came to be a livin' curse
Save that drama for your mama
Or else donate your life to the Dali Lama

An oyster spends five years digesting scum and deluge
But it can produce a pearl so beautiful and huge
My love for you got lost in its own subterfuge
I need a filter like an oyster to recycle my refuge

If you didn't spend all your time mad, you might be happy
Maybe then you wouldn't feel so crappy
You have a place in this world but it's not here
Pack your bags sugar, maybe next year

How can you hate someone you don't even know
Then say good-bye to your faithful glow
I thought you were in it for us but you were only in it for you
That's why I feel so dag gone blue

Live your life so at the end, everyone around you is cryin'
That's the way to treat the undyin'
Maybe then, we'll get back to sighin'
Dear Lord, stop my brain from this fryin'

Whatever happened to women and children first?
Me oh my came to be a livin' curse
Save that drama for your mama
Or else donate your life to the Dali Lama.

I think all the men forgot to sink with the boat so now you're stuck with us gals.
We may not be very smart but we can still lift heavy things.

U Can't Have It Both Ways

U can't have it both ways and be right
U gotta give up one of those beliefs at night
U can't have it both ways and be content
U gotta foreclose your tunnel of love for rent

U know when ur young ya want to do everythin'
The problem is u just can't afford the mess
When you're too old u can afford the dress
But your body is a conglomeration of physical distress

U can't have it both ways and be right
U gotta give up one of those beliefs at midnight
U can't have it both ways and be content
U gotta give up your tunnel of love or get all bent

U know when ur young u want to do everythin'
The problem is u just can't buy the mess
When you're too old u can buy it
But your body is an abomination of too much stress

U criticize all those who meet your jealous eyes
They all have something wrong with them
U like to point it out to the masses
But the mirror reflects its dilemma back on u

U can't have it both ways
People will see thru the travesties
They can't take any more brutalities
U can't have it both ways

U demonize all those who meet your jealous eyes
They all have somethin' wrong with their disguise
U like to point it out to the masses
But the mirror reflects its dilemma back on you

U can't have it both ways
People will see thru the irrationalities
They can't take any more calamities
U can't have it both ways.

U's Theorem of Rationality: Those who want it both ways will lose concentration
and will always end up with no ways n' lost ways.

Is it tomorrow now?

I heard a four-year old say just the other day
He woke up and yawned, 'Is it tomorrow now?'
I looked at him with a grin as I sipped my witches brew
If you only knew how much I wish that was true

Chorus
Is it tomorrow now?
My yesterday blues don't know how
This could be true
When my tomorrow time is so new

Is it tomorrow now?
Then maybe my baby would forgive me
For taken too much liberty
In this town of Schenectady.

I know it is tomorrow when I wake up today and have the Holy Ghost in my day.
This goes out to you Michael, you dinosaur-loving philosopher.

Feel Change

Feel, (Feel what?), Feel the times
Change, (Change what?), Change your ways
Move, (Move what?), Move yourself
Shake, (Shake what?), Shake them bones

Jump, (Jump where?), Jump to the moon
Dance, (Dance where?), Dance the streets
Ride, (Ride where?), Ride the mountains
Run, (Run where?), Run to her arms

Build, (Build how?), Build with your hands
Love, (Love how?), Love from within
Give, (Give how?), Give with your love
Trust, (Trust how?), Trust with faith.

A reggae dance song.

Only Time Remembers the Real Times

He remembers the good times
She remembers the bad times
Only time remembers the real times
So off they go into a worried welcoming

He remembers the full times
She remembers the hungry times
Only time remembers the real times
So there they go into a reeling rendezvous

He remembers the low times
She remembers the high times
Only time remembers the real times
So off they go into a tumultuous tirade

He remembers the hard times
She remembers the soft times
Only time remembers the real times
So there they go into an frivolous funk.

Only time can recall history with any degree of accuracy. Homo sapiens twist it into their own prejudiced reality; I'm sorry, we're bred that way.

It's Time

It's 10/4 in Baltimore
Come on baby, let's score
You need to dive on the floor
I need to provide you more

It's 20:20 in Kuala Lumpur
Volcanoes are erupting in rapture
Tsunami waves are lookin' for some destruction
Who put those volcanoes back into eruption?

It's March Fourth in Dang Valley
Once upon a time I believed in Sally
She was much more than a simple tally
Until she put me out to sea in that galley

It's 9/11 in New York City
The planes came and brought the pain
I try to find power in that disdain
In the circle of everything that became vain.

Wrote this on 10/4 as I watched a local high school volleyball game. It took off from there.

Crisis du Jour

We're livin' in a crisis du jour
I'm sick of all this and so much more
You can take your crisis du jour
And shove it up your rotten core

We're livin' in our own crisis du jour
I'm tired of this emotional bore
You can take your crisis du jour
And sledgehammer that fictitious door

We're livin' in a crisis du jour
I'm disdained by this pop-fiction folklore
You can take your crisis du jour
And go see what real people once wore

We're livin' in our own crisis du jour
I'm ridin' a thermal in a flightless soar
You can take your crisis du jour
And get ready to let out a loud roar.

Dedicated to Hollywood and the media scoundrels.

Crossroads

You're either growin' or dyin'
If you believe that then don't be cryin'
It's time to visit your crossroads
And see what tomorrow loads

I feel like a number
In a God forsaken company
Whatever happened to people make the difference?
Got replaced by a bean counter without any reference

U can tell the phase of a man by the shoes he's wearin'
That's why a barefooted Isaiah said, 'Here am I, send me'
Lead, follow or get out of the way
That's the credo of our crossroads galaxy

So you are 93 million miles from the sun
Your crossroads are about to be well done
So pick up your instrument and make a dent
Release your soul and go repent.

My ode to Robert Johnson, Henry David Thoreau and Robert Frost. Your
crossroads will come sooner or later. Make that right turn and give it all you have.

7. Sports

Marathon

Went to Steamtown to take a good day run
Man, I never had so much runnin' fun
26.2 miles through the Pocono hills
Endless mountains and small town thrills

Hit the brick wall at mile fourteen
My body said, 'No way,' to the unseen
Twelve miles of pure mind games
Those Steamtown sweethearts made me sane

They cheered for us in every small town
The high school band played music all around
The street people handed me oranges
My legs tried to keep pace with their kindness

I saw my brother at mile twenty-six
Like me, he needed a wooden crutch
For four hours we tested our wills
Runnin' through those Pennsylvania hills.

If ya want to see what's inside of you then go run a marathon. I give many thanks to my brother for the push and the small town folks cheerin' us on. I'll never forget that Carbondale high school band playin' as we ran through their Mayberry RFD streets. My most intense memory had to be a barefooted townie runnin' down the road handing out hankies to the marathoners. He reminded me of a Mississippi hippie with a heart of gold, God bless that dude.

Don't Pull the Rope

Professor Al took me on his boat
Against a muddy river, he was a giver
Showed me how to water ski
Showed me what's inside of me

Lesson number one,
Don't pull the rope
Lesson number two,
If you do,
We'll come around to get you

Lesson number three,
Study hard and you'll go far
Lesson number four,
If you do,
We'll come around to get you

Lesson number five,
Have fun and you'll be fine
Lesson number six,
If you do,
We'll come around to get you.

This is my ode to Professor Al who taught me how to water ski on the Bird River. His prized water ski came off my foot on that muddy river on Friday the 13th. It never surfaced but my appreciation to him always did. Professor Al passed in 2007 and his teachings continue in my steps today.

From Naismith to Pistol Pete

It's amazin' how a round ball
Changed so many lives
It's amazin' how a peach basket
Changed my personal life

From James Naismith to Pistol Pete
From Wilt the Stilt to my two jumpin' feet
With a leather ball that can fascinate us all
Launched thirty feet in the air with such care

Now Pistol Pete said it best when he passed away
He found God and succumbed on the basketball freeway
He said to those who could hear before he died
He said with pride, deep inside, 'I feel Great.'

This is my Ode to Basketball which changed my life for sure. Originally was goin' to be about how basketball and religion changed Pete Maravich's life then I went to thinkin', it has changed millions of lives, mine no exception. Pete's last words before passing on the basketball court resonate in his focused faith.

It's funny how a sport and faith can open so many doors, more than you can imagine. All from a game invented by a physical education teacher to keep kids active in the wintertime in Springfield, Massachusetts. My brother, cousins and I invented Skippyball; we better get that sport in gear, aye fellas?

Why Am I Livin?

I was playin' some basketball in my younger days
On the court when my life was in an early phase
The memories of runnin' the hardwood
Nothin' can take them away, not even a rainy day

One day Johnny Ro took a shot
It was a layup that rolled out of the hoop
So Johnny Ro yelled out loud,
'Why Am I Livin?'

I'll tell you why your livin' Johnny Ro
Cause you're a man destined for greatness
You're as solid as a rock and a tunnel of light
You're the rock that one can build greatness and might

Some of my best times were on the hardwood
Hangin' out with my boys and testin' our will
My stamina was built on a round ball's surface
My competition was based on this singular purpose.

I once read, 'A player that makes a team great is more valuable than a great player.'
So true.

I also heard some of the funniest things on the basketball court; things that crack me
up to this day. Johnny Ro, don't ya know, God bless. It's funny how a golf ball,
tennis ball or any other ball can dominate and change your life. Thank the caveman
and wheel next time ya see one.

Miracle in Section 34

Fans cheer and the crowds guzzle down their beer
I remember Memorial Stadium like is was still here
Just like Wild Bill who threw his cooler overboard
I was evicted once for throwin' somethin' when they scored

Now Wild Bill was the greatest fan I've ever seen
He was a cab driver by day, at night a rebel-rouser dean
When I once wore an Angels hat, I thought I was dead
He barked at me, 'Who sh*t on your head'

He led the mighty roar from Section Thirty-Four
We had Cal, Eddie, Dempsey, Flanny, Palmer and McGregor
Not to mention Earl, Singleton, Belanger and Boddicker
A bunch of baseball studs that carried a mighty moniker

By the time he spelled out O-R-I-O-L-E-S you were pumped
Now he's replaced by a bird that I want to jump
Nothin' will ever replace those days
Not even the 21st century ballpark disco haze

Wild Bill made the USA Today when he passed the other day
How many beer drinkin' fans get a spread like that you say
Only the ones that make a real difference, aye!
God Bless ya O's man, they can never take Section 34 away.

In 1986, I witnessed a sloppy drunk fan single handily start the wave at Milwaukee's County stadium. It took him four beer-soaked innings and was quite a feat but could not stand up to the longevity of another fan I came across. I had some wonderful memories watchin' the Baltimore Orioles dominate in the 70's and early 80's. We rightfully called it Orioles magic. Our best cheerleader was a fanatical cab driver in the upper deck who knew how to drink a beer and instigate a crowd. He once had 3,000 people in unison tell Reggie Jackson he was a piece of sh*t every inning he took right field. Reggie wanted a piece of him but he was no match against the mighty Hagy.

Wild Bill had his faults, but he sure was devoted and genuine. Memorial Stadium was replaced by the beautiful Camden Yards, unfortunately the blue collar fan was replaced by a brick discotheque between innings that got sucker-punched by its own curveball fate.

Rugby

Back in the day I played a few games of rugby
It sparked some high times in memory
I remember the scrum and then some
I remember scoring a try and not knowing why

Man, did those folks know the call
Of passin' the ball around in the fall
The thing I remember most though
Is the parties after the throw

To me it was like playin' tackle football
Without the pads and the stall
Like a wishbone offense on the prowl
Rugby is worth the time and the howl.

I only played three games as a teenager but I remember them well. I also remember
the nut jobs in the scrum, the parties and the high-class doctor teammates. It's not
for everyone, you may get banged up, but if your young and curious, take a peek.

Festivus Maximus

There was a Festivus Maximus among us
On a purple and black magic bus
Winter of 2000, the Ravens were diggin' in
Footballs were fallin' and we got the win

January twenty-ninth 2001 came around
We were Super Bowl and Tampa bound
A hound dog defense barked all the way there
Even the mighty Giants got done over rare

Chorus
Festivus Maximus, what a feelin'
Festivus Maximus, don't go reelin'
Festivus Maximus, keep barkin' our name
Festivus Maximus, 34 to 7, what a game

Billick and Stover got a kick
Kerry Collins took many a lick
A Dilfer and a bunch of Lewis'
We had nothin' left but hugs and kisses.

I was fortunate to live in Chicago when the Bears had the 'Super Bowl shuffle' mixed in with their Super Bowl run. Walter Peyton has to be the biggest football stud I ever saw play. With a similar Bears defense, I witnessed the Ravens display their form of physical punishment on their run to glory. Speakin' of Baltimore greats, let's pay homage to Johnny Unitas, the coolest quarterback ever. Do I need to mention he was a Lithuanian? Let's not forget Butkus either.

8. Love & Relationships

My love for you is dire
I think I'm going to expire
If I can't find my way into you
My Lithuanian soul will turn blue

Fightin' Evolution's Horny Hand

My DNA says go lay in the hay
With anything that passes this way
Go mate with everything that walks
It don't matter if it stutters when it talks

My ten commandments fight my DNA
Only time will tell who wins the match
It's a fifteen rounder with two heavyweights
I have my money on the scripture with one mate

So Darwin and the philosophers are on trial
Will my temptations last until the last mile
I've got nothin' left to do but smile, smile, smile
I still have my six-foot metal shaft pry bar to move the pile

I'm a sinner lookin' for a lonely winner
One that likes to be humble with me
One that likes to provide traceability with me
One that likes to be a full-time lover with me.

What a battle. It's playin' out every second in our society. Ya can watch it free on the news or pay for it on the dark side of the avenue.

She's My Rock

Some people rely on sand to hold them up
Only to find out they sink when life shifts their cup
Ah, my woman let's me put down a foundation
That could outlast any God-hating nation

She's my rock cause I need a foundation
Someone to hold my hand in my trepidation
Ah, she's bound to make a better man of me
Take my pebble and turn it to granite vivaciously

Some people rely on false promises to get them by
Only to find out they got nothing when it goes dry
Ah, my woman lets me put down a foundation
That could outlast any God-hating nation

She's my rock cause I need a foundation
Someone to hold my hand in my trepidation
Ah, she's bound to make a better man of me
Take my granite and let me be free.

Hopefully you have a rock to provide you support in a shifting sands world.

The Foundation

Without a foundation, the triangle would crumble
Without a foundation, the righteous would stumble
Without a foundation, the poets would bumble
Without a foundation, my love for you would tumble

Without a foundation, the house would crumble
Without a foundation, the peaceful would rumble
Without a foundation, Walter Peyton would fumble
Without a foundation, Bryant Gumble would mumble

Without a foundation, the terrorist would be humble
Without a foundation, the jigsaw would jumble
Without a foundation, the mime would mumble
Without a foundation, this poem would crumble.

Without a foundation, my infrastructure would succumb to the babblin' bum.

If Mama Ain't Happy

If Mama ain't happy, nobody's happy
If Mama ain't happy, nobody's happy
If Mama ain't happy, Daddy ain't happy

If ya want to make Mama happy
Go out and buy her some fudge
If ya want to make Mama happy
Give her a three-week vacation

If Mama ain't happy, nobody's happy
If Mama ain't happy, nobody's happy
If Mama ain't happy, the kids ain't happy

If ya want to make Mama happy
Go out and get her a massage
If ya want to make Mama happy
Give her a bouquet of carnations

If Mama ain't happy, nobody's happy
If Mama ain't happy, nobody's happy
If Mama ain't happy, the dogs ain't happy

If ya want to make Mama happy
Go out and write her a poem
If ya want to make Mama happy
Give her all your considerations

If Mama ain't happy, nobody's happy
If Mama ain't happy, nobody's happy
If Mama ain't happy, nobody's happy.

Dedicated this song to my spouse who's in the house. Words and tune came easily after watchin' Pastor Arnold Murray talk about what's important in the family. Mixes well with an organ, bass, children voices and a slide trombone.

Beauty, Truth and Knowledge

She's got beauty, truth and knowledge
She's got beauty, truth and knowledge
It's the softest kiss which produces the most intense feelin'
That's when your beauty begins to healin'

She's got beauty, truth and knowledge
She's got beauty, truth and knowledge
It's the lightest touch which produces the most intense feelin'
That's when your truth begins to dealin'

She's got beauty, truth and knowledge
She's got beauty, truth and knowledge
It's the kindest words which produce the most intense feelin'
That's when your knowledge begins to peelin'.

Dedicated to the holy trinity of my soul partner.

I Do – Redo

Many years after we tie the knot
I want to do an I do, redo
That's right
I want to do an I do, redo

For richer, for poorer
That's what we pledged on our weddin' day
Twenty years later
I want to do an I do, redo

In sickness and in health
That's what we pledged on our weddin' day
Forty years later
I want to do an I do, redo

For trust and not lust
That's what we pledged on our weddin' day
Sixty years later
I want to do an I do, redo.

Ah, the multi-year renewal of vows. Some live in the now, some live for commitment, some wonder how. This is for the spouse. We have forty more years to go darlin'.

Sisters

They call her Full Moon Molly
Blond hair and full of oh my golly
She made the world around her jolly
Just like the song, 'Well Hello Dolly'

They call her Entertaining Emily
Brown hair and livin' life free
I used to rock her on my bendin' knee
Now she's old enough to climb her own tree

There's nothin' like sister love
Sharin' emotions from deep above
Their hands fit like two gloves
There's nothin' like sister love.

Dedicated to two sisters livin' the high life in the 16 acre outback.

Body Parts

I saw a bumper sticker the other day
'I have over 230 joints in my body
But not one I can smoke with you'
Ah, come on now, it ain't that bad

I have 650 muscles in my body
Ten fingers and ten crooked toes
And one very large nose
But I have one hundred wishes for you

I have 206 bones in my body
Seven layers of a weathered epidermis
And one thought about a lost miss
But I have one thousand thoughts about you

I have one brain in my body
Two ears and some brass knuckles
And one thought about a high school chuckle
But I have one million grins about you.

You can donate kidneys and other body parts. Man can also manufacture bones of titanium so one can walk again. You can do all these things but they can not manufacture and demonstrate my love for you.

That's Where They Go Pokin'

Just remember, when ya start to slackin'
Get off your ass and just get to crackin'
Get on the baseball diamond and start smackin'
Hit it over the wall and go whackin'

Just remember, when ya start to jokin'
Get some new pipes and don't go tokin'
Get some Cubans and then go smokin'
Over there, that's where they go pokin'

Just remember, when ya start to creakin'
Get some oil before ya start to leakin'
Get some lips before ya start to speakin'
Take your clothes off and then go streakin'

Just remember, when ya start to jokin'
Get some chicken and don't go chokin'
Get some bullfrogs and then go croakin'
Over there, that's where they go pokin'.

Sometimes ya just have to poke around if ya want to see what's livin' underground.

9. Nature

So I came across some undulations long ago.

Oceans covered landforms of past
Exploding mountains in the sky
Carving canyons incredibly fast
Cro-Magnon lived only to die.

Something was cooking 543 million years in the know.

In the amoebae-laden water came us all
Struggling to land with primeval fins
Breathing air and hearing the sudden call
Of woolly mammoth crying his 1,000 sins.

Hemlock Gorge

I took a trip the other day to one of my favorite places
A place filled with ancient hemlocks in a timeless gorge
A place so gorgeous only God could have created
With its waters flowing over rocky precipices I traversed

When ya look up ya better count your blessings
I don't think that sky of blue can penetrate you
It's so dark and mysterious in Hemlock Gorge
Ya better be careful when ya cross the brook in forge

It takes a special environment for the Hemlock Gorge
They only grow where time keeps hidden secrets
It's a curious place indeed
When ya sit under these majestic trees

I heard someone sing the other day
They would rather be in some dark hollow
If this is true and your time is overdue
Then the place to go is Hemlock Gorge.

My two favorite hemlock gorges are at Prettyboy Reservoir and a track near the
Susquehanna River. Being in a Hemlock Gorge is like being in an altered state of
consciousness. If you've never been, go seek refuge in a Hemlock Gorge.

Dense Fog

Have you ever been in a fog so dense you couldn't see?
Believe you me, I had such a travesty
It was not in San Francisco but in Chicago
Couldn't see your hand one foot in front of you

Had nothin' but faith to pull me through
When ya can't see the physical ya need a logical clue
Whether ya have the Bible or Darwin's natural selection
Find your favorite verse and repeat after me

Chorus
I have a dense fog in front of me
I'm in dense fog and I can't see
Was blinded but now I believe
That dense fog put a spell on me

Have you ever been in a fog so dense you couldn't see?
Believe you me, I had such a travesty
It was not in Singapore but in Baltimore
Couldn't see your hand one foot in front of you.

Something heavy, something light, that dense fog will envelope you one of these nights. Make sure you have your fog lights and an open mind or you may perish.

Second Wind

So tired from runnin' I gotta sit down
My old bones need a rest before I get back around
Sometimes I need a prayer then I'll be fine
Sometimes I need a glass of cabernet wine
Then I'll get my second wind n' come around

So tired from hangin' out I gotta sit down
My old bones need a massage before I get back around
Sometimes I need a prayer then I'll be fine
Sometimes I need to go n' walk the line
Then I'll get my second wind n' come around

So tired from thinkin' I gotta sit down
My old bones need a break before I get back around
Sometimes I need a prayer then I'll be fine
Sometimes I need to study the vines
Then I'll get my second wind n' come around

So tired from plantin' I gotta sit down
My old bones need a reprieve before I get back around
Sometimes I need a prayer then I'll be fine
Sometimes I need to count to ninety-nine
Then I'll get my second wind n' come around.

This is dedicated to the Dave Wottle 1972 Olympic kick. I remember watchin' that stud run with that hat of his in Munich. That dude knew how to finish a race after he gracefully received and believed in his second wind.

Oak Tree

Ol' man winter comes 'round with a brisk wind
Every now and then a snow-burst colors it white
I see an evergreen and many bare timber
But the one that always sticks out is the oak tree

Its top leaves have fallen softly to the ground
Leavin' the ones on lower limbs dearly holdin' on
He reminds me of a weathered old man
With a bald head and a beard of leaves

Chorus
The stronger the wind, the stronger the tree
The bigger the tree, the bigger the trunk
The bigger the trunk, the deeper the roots
The deeper the roots, the stronger the tree

Spring comes 'round my place with a March wind
Every now and then a raindrop colors it green
I see rainbows and the lofty limbs
Ol' man oak's bald head starts fillin' in

His green leaves make him look young again
He's got wood that's upright and strong
His nuts remind me of a rejuvenated ol' man
With a luscious head and a beard of green.

Next winter, take a look around for that bald-headed, bearded oak tree. Once ya
find him, send him my love. I bet he'll be smilin' back at you.

That Special Place and a Peace of Mind

James Taylor went up on the roof
David Letterman went on the goof
Jacques Cousteau went under the water
Bob Gibson went on the mound as a starter

Chorus
Everyone has a special place
To get a peace of mind
Everyone has a special face
To share along with mankind

Bob Dylan went out on the stage
Count Dracula went on a rage
Benton MacKaye went in the woods
The Dutch went out to trade some goods

Everyone has a special place
To get a peace of mind
Everyone has a special face
To share along with mankind.

I know where my special places are: In the house with the kids and spouse, ridin' a
bicycle up a hill, Hamlin Beach State Park, in the Vineyard, the Appalachian Trail,
doin' suicides on a basketball court, Memorial Stadium, Hemlock Gorge,
Lutherville Woods, they all got the goods on me. I hope you visit yours when the
wind blows.

Ursus maritimus

There's somethin' white on that horizon
It can float on an iceberg and weigh half a ton
It's a polar bear and he looks hungry
Hungry enough to catch a seal and devour me

Ursus maritimus
Got caught up in a big fuss
With an Eskimo on the tundra land
One filled with many a frozen fish gland

I often wonder how they stand the cold
Adaptation taken into another fold
I would die in a minute or two
If I had to put up with the Arctic wind blowin' anew

Ursus maritimus
Ended up north marveling everyone of us
Including an Eskimo on the tundra land
One filled with many a frozen fish gland.

Felt compelled to honor one of my favorite animals. They are a clever animal and
have adapted well to the brutal elements. I must also add the one-horned rhinoceros
to my marveled species list.

Bullfrogs and Honey Bees

I wanna be near the bullfrogs and honey bee
Please appease me under this flowering tree
I'll get down on my knees and say my ABC's
If ya only let me hear the lovely songs and Z's

One croaks and the other one does a buzz
One swims in the pond just because
One makes honeycomb and has a fuzz
They both are from a land that once was

I wanna be near the honey bee and bullfrogs
On a farm with our sheepdogs and hogs
I see the honeybees livin' in the logs
And the bullfrogs matin' in the bogs.

There are 50,000 honeybees in the average hive; don't dress in black or they will think you're Satan. A female bullfrog lays 10,000 eggs, of which a few will be lucky to breathe air. We're not makin' it any easier for them.

If these two wonderful creatures exit before Homo sapiens, we're in deep trouble.

24 Hours to Live

I have 24 hours to live
I'm a mayfly and I'm lookin' for a siv
If you're receptive, I have somethin' to give
Come to my lily pad and let me live

I have 12 hours to fly
I need a young lady to sigh
I'm hopin' loud and proud, me oh my
I hope she gives me another try

I have 4 hours to succumb
Listen gal, I'm no bum
If ya want me, bang my drum
I'll make you coo and hum

I have 10 minutes to expire
I just became a true daddy sire
Our mayfly baby will put out the fire
When he has his 24 hours to retire.

Mayflies live for only one day or twenty-four hours. Do ya think they sit on the couch with the remote? Hell no, they have one thing in mind. I'm sure ya know what that is.

The World of Hybrids

I'm livin' in a world of hybrids
Makes me want to blink my eyelids
Golf clubs, cars and plastic surgery
All take this life into another reality

I'm livin' in a world of hybrids
Ya mix it up with the kids
I saw a picture of a lion-tiger hybrid boss
Made the liger look like a king of the cross

If ya look far enough back I guess we're all hybrids
I say this when lookin' at the evolution grids
Ya mix it all up and fusion will take over
That's what the three said to the four-leaf clover

I'm livin' in a world of hybrids
Makes me want to blink my eyelids
Golf clubs, cars and plastic surgery
All take this life into another reality.

Amalgam and ponder on this one my friend.

10. Science

Humans came along and determined the race.

Sharp spear point javelined into space
Squarely sinking our woolly friend
Erupting a smile from the hunter's face
This wound would never mend.

Manifest destiny left us on a mission to space.

Expanding across wide open land
Climate and stars causing superstitions
And knowledge coming from his hand
Spaceships were built for the continued missions.

Cosmic Collisions

I see an axis tilted years ago by time zero
I see a moon with craters and a face
I see the evidence of explosions in space
It boomed in a big bang billions of years ago

I take my telescope and point it high in the sky
I see quasars, comets and constellations
I see a universe expanding its rays
I see the evidence of this every day

I embrace my astronomy and wonder why I try
I see a moon formed from a colossal crash
I see cosmic collisions creating a new genus
I see the evidence of this in a fiery Venus

I see stars, constellations and galaxies
I see cosmic collisions forming new dimensions
I see the evidence of this in universal tensions
It boggles my mind how space reveals time.

Look through your trifocals, there's a kite, no it's a plane, no it's the Andromeda Galaxy. Some say one day our galaxies will pull towards each other and create a wonderful new world. Hold on tight cause cosmic collisions have a way of re-creating life. Inspiration came from watchin' Robert Redford narrate Cosmic Collisions while visiting the Air and Space Museum in Washington, DC.

Einstein

Einstein once said
'Science without religion is lame
Religion without science is blind'
I say, use your non-conformance to make a find

Chorus
Einstein and 1905
An outcast Jew who knew the clue
A magical year in relativity
Changed the world with his rhapsody

He said, 'Imagination is more important than knowledge'
By studying time and space with a new view
That's what he relayed to us years ago
He was a self-taught genius in the know

Einstein was like a complex wine
Blended and produced theories for all mankind
Ones that would bend your simple mind
Ones that would give the universe a new baby's behind.

Arguably the greatest non-conformist of his generation. This was probably his supreme strength. He could think outside of the box and boy did he ever. He spent his later years trying to place the universe into a unified field theory but ran out of the one thing he understood well, Swiss time.

Time Zero – Part One

Who's your hero?
Is it Osama Bin Laden or Time Zero?
Is it Satan or Emperor Nero?
Look to your past and provide us your answer

Chorus
Every big has a bang
Every ying has a yang
Every George has a dang
Oooh we, ya gotta love that bang

Who's your hero?
Is it Abraham Lincoln or Time Zero?
Is it Almighty God or Robert De Niro?
Look to your past and provide us your answer.

What is a God to do in the empty spaces of the universe?

Even though white holes have not been proven to exist yet, I submit they one day will and our big bang could be theorized into this phenomenon. We'll have to ride a worm hole back in time to find out. Make it so.

A close cousin of Cosmic Collisions. So what do you think was goin' down at Time Zero, Part One?

Time Zero – Part Two

Some say billions of years from now
Our universe will collapse and take a bow
They call it the Big Rip
Cause the Big Bang already took grip

Chorus
Every big has a rip
Every trip has a blip
Every faucet has a drip
Oooh we, ya gotta loathe that rip

Dark Energy has a spell on me
It takes a shape that I can't see
I see it has a force on relativity
Oh Lord, this is the biggest mystery.

I think if this was my theory, I would have coined it, 'The Big Fookin'
Decompression.' I stood next to eternity but couldn't accept it.

There's the Book of Revelations, Global Warming and the Book of Dark Energy.
Einstein predicted the latter in 1917 but later abandoned it. His greatest
withdrawals are our greatest ideas. Since it has never been directly detected, we
still are working on this complicated puzzle.

It all goes back to this stuff we can't see called Dark Energy. It's gravity's
competition. Like God and Satan, Republicans and Democrats, the Yankees and
Red Sox. It's amazing we've gone 4 billion years without one of them destroying
the other.

Don't worry, our future grandthings may have 20 billion years, give or take, to
figure it all out. I suspect divine intervention will make a stand. Just remember, the
first messenger is supposed to be a trickster.

Quantum Gravity

I don't know much about quantum gravity
Just that is has a force over you and me
When they solve the theory to everything
Do ya think God will come down and sing?

Many have tried to unify the physics of the universe
Only to find out it has a complexity beyond their reality
Quantum fields, particle beams, general and special relativity
Theoretical physics, microscopic length scales and unbridled energy

When I get old and downright dreary
I pray we have a Grand Unified Theory
It's all in the gravitons I do declare
Unifying quantum mechanics over a split hair.

One of quantum gravity goals is a unified framework for all fundamental forces - a
'theory of everything', or 'Grand Unified Theory (GUT)'. So whoever can
harmonize relativity to quantum mechanics wins the prize. It will have to be
someone who knows about curvatures in space time, string theories, singularities,
black holes, white holes, worm holes, magnetic poles, quantum mechanics and
above all, non-conformance. Question is, will it be a simple or elegant theory?
Examine your GUT and microscopes to find out.

The Prime Directive

I have too much scientist in me
To let false emotions control my deity
So Gene Rodenberry created the Star Trek mission
Used a transporter and nuclear fission

Some people believe in the Prime Directive
Some people believe in being selective
Some people get relief in non-interference
Some people get relief in building a fence

The prime directive was with the Star Trek Crew
Starfleet's General Order #1 as they flew
No interference, no hanky pank
If you do, you lose your rank

Some people believe in the Prime Directive
Some people believe in the Borg Collective
Some people get relief in non-interference
Some people get relief in social nonsense.

Ah, Starfleet's guiding principle which can lead to a paradoxical situation. Some say you're a wimp if you refuse to act. Others say you don't have the right to impose your beliefs on the locals and you're messin' with temptation. Should your country or you embrace this? Do you enjoy gettin' up in someone's grill? Whatever happened to Westphalian sovereignty?

I think Einstein's equation said it well:

If A is success in life, then A equals X plus Y plus Z.

Work is X; Y is Play; and Z is keeping your mouth shut.

Then I saw bumper sticker from God that hit me square in the face:
Except for ending slavery, fascism, Nazism and communism, war has never solved anything.

From the walls of Jericho to the walls of the iron curtain, all walls must eventually come down.

I'm De-Evolving

When you've got poison in your body streams
Ya got poison in your unsettled dreams
I'll never forget the one that almost did me in
It was a New Hampshire summer to remember

The heat was about and my head was steamin'
I lay in bed and my spirits went to dreamin'
My body took the most primitive form around
I became a paramecium in a one-cell town

I turned and turned until God gave me three outs
I was like a Borg in the collective filled with group doubt
If I left the hive would the evolution of life stop with me?
A one-cell paramecium, full of too much delirium

The sweat poured out of my body in despair
When I transformed I said to myself with so much care
I've de-evolved to the paramecium and know the code
It's all about the needs of the many outweigh the needs of the one.

The spark for this came from a dream I had in the Hampshire wilds.

Astronomy

Globular cluster in circumstance
A binary star attraction
The grand distances to be scaled
By parallax and radiation

Gliding on the hot-air rising
Forming clouds on the fringe
Of this mediocre sphere
In this mediocre galaxy

And yes I demand the truth
Don't turn your head to the science
The complexities do grow
And your insignificance seeps on through

Yea, we're not the center of mother universe
And man the dominant is in his curse
It's a hard line but it's alright
Take heed of our brutal past and the future fight

Our race is getting too much control
Maybe some androids will inherit a soul
A decrease in numbers will succumb
I'm placing my bets on the troubled some.

This poem and 'Jesus Saves' were the only poems put to paper prior to 2007; both were written in my college days. The influence for this poem was a summer college course in Astronomy. That teacher had me on the edge of my chair the whole time he lectured. He would make Carl Sagan happy.

Rocks

Time reveals itself in the rocks
Geologists use them as the history clocks
Sedimentary, Igneous and Metamorphic
Pressurized, heated and squeezed in a petrified shtick

Shale, sandstone, limestone and gypsum
Magma, basalt, granite and obsidian
Marble, quartz, schist and slate
Plate tectonics gave them an origin and a fate

Millions of years ago a crash happened in Gondwanaland
Pangaea ripped apart and collided creating the Appalachians
Now we study the rocks to help solve the mystery
And they provide quite a story of our ancient history

Time reveals itself in the rocks
Geologists use them as the history clocks
Sedimentary, Igneous and Metamorphic
Drifted, uplifted and squeezed in a stony shtick.

So if you believe in the geological time scale, Earth is 4.6 billion years old. If you fit this into a 24 hour day, 23 hours and 58 minutes would be void of man. Hmmm.

According to the rocks, modern life started 543 million years ago. That leaves over 3 billion years that our cousins, primitive bacteria and algae, ruled the roost. Think about that the next time you're lookin' at the green scum of a pond. Maybe God was taking a nap, but I suspect the magnetic force was out there creating the rest of its masterpiece.

If you know plate tectonics and a thing about crust and dust, you know a lot about creation, destruction and movement. Take a voyage to the Grand Canyon rocks if ya want to get a sense of this mystery.

Ode to all the Ologists

Some study a long time to achieve a professional degree
They do much science and philosophy

Give thanks to the Geologists
Don't forget the Anthropologists, Archeologists and Zoologists
Give praise to the Epidemiologists
Don't forget the Radiologists, Urologists and Pathologists

Some seek truth in what has been
They do much science and heal society

Give thanks to the Geologists
Don't forget the Anthropologists, Archeologists and Zoologists
Give praise to the Anesthesiologists
Don't forget the Hematologist, Cardiologists and Proctologists

Some seek truth in what will be
They do much science and chemistry.

Ya need to send a card to your favorite *ologist* and thank them for their
contributions to society and making this a better place to live. That includes your
Proctologist from Dover who said bend over Rover while I look for that four-leaf
clover.

A self-portrait menagerie of calamity and ink dots drawn in 1983 from a questioning 19 year-old roaming the Southwest. This is what 23 straight days sleeping under the desert stars in a geological time scale will do to a free, Lithuanian mind.

13. Nonsense

Rhymes

Yo, know your glow when you row, sow and go blow
Place your face in case the mace defines your baseless race
Care with long hair from a short stare at the state fair
From a dumb bum I would succumb with a hitch-hikin' thumb

Y'all play ball in the fall with the tall from the hall
Call your town mall doll cause y'all have a brick-wall stall
Loan the stoned drone and throw him another bone
Atone peasants and the pine cone will moan to the drone

Honeybee go find a tree so you and me can find relativity
See if your reality will be reset in a two-part harmony
Free your society of a workin' fatality in reality
Be free from calamity and save your fragile mentality.

Yo, so ya know how to rhyme in time now go flow your glow cause you're in the know.

What Would Scooby-doo Do?

I'm atomically attracted to you
I'm biologically attracted to you
I'm chemically attracted to you
My only question in suspension
What the hoot would Scooby-doo do?

What would Jesus do?
What would Abe Lincoln do?
What would George Washington do?
What would Sherlock Holmes do?
My only question in suspension
What the toot would Scooby-doo do?

I'm astrologically attracted to you
I'm bucolically attracted to you
I'm charmingly attracted to you
My only question in suspension
What the hoot would Scooby-doo do?

What would Fred do?
What would Daphne do?
What would Velma do?
What would Shaggy do?
My only question in suspension
What the toot would Scooby-doo do?

Scooby-doo where the hoot are you? I have some Scooby snacks for you. This goes out to Kelly, Lucky and Seven. Next to my soul partner, you're my best friend.

Pigeon-Free Liberty

Pigeons jostle on the historic monuments
They defecate on General Grant's head and he can relate
He just waits for the rain to wash it free
Whatever happened to pigeon-free liberty?

I see a broken mirror in the park
It's in a thousand pieces and shattered all about
It still has the audacity to reflect back on me
Even though I'm livin' in a multi-part travesty

There's people livin' in this park they call home
Don't feel too sorry cause they enjoy its company
They have squirrels to feed and friends in need
They dream and sleep and dream of yesteryear's creed.

Inspiration came from Farragut Park in DC but I wanted to plug General Grant.
Guns down, that soldier wrote the best personal memoir every conceived, who
would of ever guessed.

Now if I can just keep the pigeons from defecating all over my barn, I'll be alright.

Harmonica Street Gal

She came on my train
Like a beautiful bum in vain
She went on a ramblin'
My brain started to descramblin'

She said how she played for her grandma
When she was five she was a star
She could play a jazz piano
And sing a wonderful soprano

She then pulled out her shiny, long harmonica
In my head I was thinkin' her name was Veronica
Everthin' she owned was in that shopping cart
When she played, she tugged at my heart

Harmonica Street Gal, you're on your way
Thank you for bringing me joy today
You gave me a smile that will forever stick
Harmonica Street Gal, you play a wonderful lick.

This street gal was on that Red Line DC Metro Train to nowhere one mornin'. She liked talkin' about when those Saints Go Marchin' In and stories of years gone by. I noticed most of the street people have a tale about their younger days when the world was a much kinder place. They talk to themselves out loud; they have nothin' to hide like you and me.

Most people don't pay attention to these folks. I can't help but get mesmerized in what they're sayin' and playin'. When she startin' blowin' that harmonica, oh boy, my heart started to pumpin'. God bless ya sweetheart.

Why do Men have Goobers?

I once knew a woman down at the steel mill
She cried out 'Balls!' every time things took a spill
It's suffice to say I heard this three times a day
My co-worker had it hard on the Chesapeake Bay

Every time somethin' she knew went a wry
My friend called out 'Balls!' and wondered why
Every time somethin' she knew went kapootz
My friend called out 'Balls!' to her metallic roots

Baseball, football and basketball had nothin' on her
She knew how balls stood up on their walls
Volleyball, softball, skippyball cried to the wind
Cause her generation of balls took one too many freefalls.

AC/DC had a good song about balls. This is dedicated to a lovely lady who I worked with years ago.

My first novel of 101 poemplanations ended with a question, Why do Men have Nipples? To make sure the space time continuum is not upset, this one ends with a similar question that came to me in a nutty prophecy.

We started with passions and ended with this fascinating goobers question. I'll keep pokin' around the bend and see if I can find a poemplanation creation to send to your favorite station.

As always, my purgin' is over, my oh me, I feel like I just went speakin' across the galaxy. I godda get my space suit back on, mow a paradoxical peace sign on my front lawn and get ready for a new dawn.

Keep on keepin' on and love hard and long. Take out your piano and write us a new song.

My science tells me how, my faith tells my why, now it's time to bid you goodbye.

Ačiū, laimingas takas!

Epilogue

Decommission Statement

I've been a Homo sapien for forty-four years
Now it's time to face all those fears
Billions of years from now on my geological clock
My skeleton will be fossilized into a metamorphic rock

According to some my soul will still be moving
My holy spirit will still be grooving
My Lithuanian karma floating in space
Looking to support another lost race

So I have a dream of buyin' some tap shoes
I want to tap dance to a bass riff singin' the blues
I want to move my feet as fast as I can
Then I will forgive every man in the fryin' pan

I came to believe in a power in the midnight hour
A power that can decommission me in a flamin' tower
Now I know to never let that power go astray
Because then my time will skip a beautiful day.

What is truth? Sometimes ya just have to let it all Dang out.

www.ingramcontent.com/pod-product-compliance
Lightning Source LLC
Chambersburg PA
CBHW032008040426

42448CB00006B/532